Essence of Our Humanity

ALSO BY NANCY JOHNSON

Letters from Egypt: Four Years of Family Life Beneath The Pyramids

In Gratitude for Life, Love, Family & Friends:
A Collection of Essays and Poems

Essence of Our Humanity

Portraits of My Beloved
Psychiatric Patients

By Nancy Johnson

Essence of Our Humanity: Portraits of My Beloved Psychiatric Patients. Copyright © 2025 by Nancy Johnson. All rights reserved. Printed in the United States of America. No part of this book may be used or reproduced in any manner whatsoever without written permission except in the case of brief quotations embedded in critical articles and reviews. For information, address Panhandle Creek Press, 107 Yatasi Court, Red Feather Lakes, Colorado, 80545.

First Edition

Illustrations and design by
Carmel Mawle

North Fork Publishing

Contents

Preface	ix
Isaac	1
Paulette	3
Peggy	5
Heather	7
Irene	9
Florence	11
Harold	13
Neil	15
Sherbert	17
Rule	19
Leonicia	21
Freddie	22
Patrick	24
Earnest	27
Natalie	29
Robert	31
Robert B.	33
Beulah	35
John	37
Afterword	39
Acknowledgements	41
About the Author	43

To all those who live with, love, or care for the mentally ill.

Preface

It was late summer in Lafayette, Louisiana – warm, but whispers of cooler days ahead. Glancing through the paper, I noticed a help wanted ad from the psychiatric hospital, looking for PRN nurses (*pro re nata* – Latin for "as needed") to cover for vacationing or ill nurses.

With my husband still working and our four children off exploring the world, I was suffering from empty nest syndrome, so I applied. As a registered nurse, I had some psychiatric training, but not much. The hospital didn't mind my inexperience, as they hired me immediately.

Located on the edge of town in a beautiful wooded area, the psychiatric hospital didn't treat violent patients. Most were being treated with psychiatric medications, individual counseling, and group therapy. At that time, restraints or solitary confinement were rarely used, and only when needed to ensure patient or staff safety. Since the 1980's, when I wrote these portraits, many new and more effective drugs have been developed and we ow understand that homosexuality, falls into the spectrum of human sexuality, rather than considered a mental illness.

My first day was a quick introduction to the various treatment programs. I was first assigned to the children's ward. On entering, I was confronted with a ten-year-old screaming, kicking, and clawing at the door to get out. Thankfully, another nurse brought a syringe with something to calm him down.

I felt helpless and overwhelmed, questioning whether this was the right job for me. The administration responded by assigning me to the teenagers. That was worse. It seemed like half of them were there just to get out of school. I didn't feel qualified to help them (or, didn't want to deal with teens).

Desperate for help, the hospital transferred me to the adult unit – the perfect fit. I was asked to conduct a group therapy meeting, so I gathered the patients to the conference room. But, outside, it was a glorious. Trees were in full bloom: cypress, redbuds, loblolly pines – Spanish moss gently draping over all. Wildflowers covered the forest floor and, much like my patients, adapted to their environment, growing, and blooming however they were able.

"Why not take a short walk outside through the forest?" I asked. The patients agreed, so out we went. Some picked flowers, others seemed happy to admire the foliage. One patient picked a leaf off a tree and stared at it, stroking it gently.

In retrospect, I probably shouldn't have taken that risk, but God saw to it that we all got back safely. When we resumed our meeting inside, I think everyone was more inclined to share. One patient, who had severely stabbed his own penis, admitted he'd done so because he'd been unfaithful to his wife. The pain of his injury, he felt, had slightly lifted the burden of his guilt.

Working with these patients was humbling, fascinating, sad, frustrating, and (sometimes) humorous. I hope that by writing about my patients, they won't be completely forgotten by the world.

Now, let me introduce you to some of my beloved patients.

Isaac

Down the hall he shuffles, 27 years old, man-boy, painfully aware that he is condemned to a lifetime of living in institutions. He spears you with his dark brown, liquid eyes. "Look at me – I have the power. Look into my eyes. Can you see the power?" He flaps his arms. "Do you see my wings? I'm Gabriel." He reaches out with his tremulous hands and gently touches a nurse's blonde hair. "I have the power to change your hair to gold – spun gold." He softly touches his finger to her forehead. "I will write my name on your forehead, so you will be taken up when Jesus comes."

He asks her to talk to him. "I want to tell you about my mother. She's a tiny thing," and he indicates a height of about three feet. "I'm breast-feeding her."

"You mean she's breast-feeding you?" she asks.

"Oh yes," he says.

Paulette

"I'm Satan's daughter, and I'm afraid I'm going to hurt the little girl." The "little girl" refers to her 21-year-old roommate, a small slender woman, lethargic from an overdose of lithium. So Paulette's room is searched, and no weapons of any consequence are unearthed.

Paulette, a large black woman in her mid-thirties, was sexually molested by her father, uncle, and brother. Her way of ridding herself of the hurt and anger and pain has been by purging, after which she feels much better. Her anger and pain spill out. She is wretched.

She talks of her beloved dog, Socks, and a big grin spreads across her face. She has never had a lover, a child. Her father has seen to that.

Peggy

"You're the biggest, fattest, white woman I've ever seen," she says to a slender nurse walking by her down the hall. "Come see what I did." She displays the toilet bowl and a goodly amount of stool in the form of large marbles. "See," she says proudly, "It took me thirty minutes to make these." Her stomach is huge, and she's not sure what's in it. "Maybe they's a baby in here," she chortles.

She comes roaring out of her room at 2:30 AM, yelling and disoriented. We are unable to calm her, so she is led into the Behavioral Control Room (BCR) where she is isolated, but can be observed by nursing staff. After she's given a sedative, she finally falls asleep.

The next morning, Peggy is somewhat subdued. She perks up during the afternoon, and by evening she is entertaining the nurses and her peers by dancing and singing "Achey Breakey Heart," a la Billy Rae Cyrus.

Heather

The splash of bright red lipstick applied carelessly to her lips looks like a gash across her pale face. Her brassy blonde hair is frizzed from repeated permanents. She's a tough little thing; her muscular legs propel her down the hall. At fifteen years old, she's a worldly girl, having been found in bed with one of her male peers. And just to ensure her sexuality, she went to bed with another one.

One wonders why, until one meets her mother in her tight shorts and body-clinging shirt that says, "I can go from nice to bitch in twenty seconds."

Irene

She stands in her room, looking vacantly at the clothes she has taken out of her drawers and folded neatly in piles. She is tall, extremely thin, and heavily wrinkled. Her lips are a thin line, sunken into her face. Her teeth are gone and she has no dentures.

When she first came to our unit a week ago, she was able to respond to questions, make decisions, albeit slowly and with some hesitation. Now, after a possible stroke, she seems inert – unable to answer a question or make a decision (would you like to go outside?).

So, she stands in her room with her nightgown on, looking at her clothes.

Florence

"Charlie, Charlie, Charlie, Charlie," reverberates down the hall, a sad, haunting, sound. Florence is calling the name of her son into the telephone receiver. She hasn't dialed, so all that can be heard is a dial tone. Her hands are shaking and she begins to cry.

She's a 63-year-old woman that looks 75, until you look at her smooth, unwrinkled skin. She's been schizophrenic for many years, and is deteriorating. When she last stayed with us, only a few months ago, she was able to care for herself, walk without assistance, and carry on a conversation, albeit somewhat stilted. Now, she is constantly lying down on the floor – anywhere. She just, all of a sudden, lies down and starts to moan.

The other patients have learned to step over her. Visitors are not quite so nonchalant.

Harold

Harold is 10 years old. He is pale and thin, with delicate hands and fingers. He has patches of ringworm on his face and body.

Harold is in four-point restraint, writhing and straining against the leather cuffs that bind his hands, wrists, and ankles.

He spews foul language no 10-year-old should know.

Neil

He's 29, his blonde hair is thinning on top. His trousers hang off his derriere. Neil's brain is fried. He's been a junkie for years. Track marks on his arms testify to that fact. That wonderful, God-given, computer we call a brain has short circuited.

He tries to connect to others on a basic level, but it doesn't always work. He's confused, and very, very sad. At times he's cognizant of what he's done to himself and his family, and he cries.

Neil has come back to us three times. He's an enigma. Maybe his brain isn't fried. After he's been with us several weeks, he can become quite sociable.

Sherbert

What a wonderful name! Sherbert is tall and thin. I guess you'd have to call him licorice Sherbert because he's black as can be.

He's an emaciated man in his 40s. Old devil drink has ravaged his body and mind.

Rule

"See, I can't stop shaking," and he holds up a severely palsied hand. Even his arms are shaking. "I'm here to get my medications adjusted," he says.

Then he starts talking, and you know for sure he's here for other reasons, as well. He starts speaking faster and faster, with a constant flight of ideas.

He likes to get right close to you when he's talking – too close for our cultural comfort. As you back away, he follows like a shadow. Still talking about things you cannot understand, in a language all his own.

If asked, he will go get himself a cup of coffee, and you make your escape. However, coffee in hand, he finds you again, and begins his unfathomable narrative.

Leonicia

An old French woman who, when asked to clean her "monkey," washes her genitals. She is wheelchair bound, but there is nothing wrong with her mouth.

She spends most of the day talking with her own ghosts.

Freddie

At 29, Freddie has a handsome face, with a café au lait complexion and large brown eyes, wide-set like a deer's. He is huddled in a corner, wrapped in a blanket, turning away from all who approach. Freddie is unresponsive to anything but the demons in his head.

Later, Freddie paces up and down the hall. He has the body of an athlete, well-developed, muscled, and a proud, easy gait. He can now acknowledge the presence of others.

His demons still haunt him. He talks about how his nephew will die, his sister will be punished, and includes various veiled threats toward hospital personnel.

He displays ritualistic behaviors. His wet socks are placed just so on the radiator; his belt was found in the garbage container in the lounge. Getting him to take his medication is a challenge. It takes thirty minutes for him to crush his pill, mix it with a certain amount of water, and stir a specified number of times. Parts of the ritual are repeated several times.

Staff is greatly relieved when he finally drinks the water in which his crushed medication resides. He would be just about ready to drink it, when he would think of some other ritual which must be performed.

Patrick

Black leather beret, an earring in one lobe, tight leather pants that encase his almost plump derriere, and a nondescript sweater setting the background for a myriad of gold chains, Patrick minces down the hall. He is an admitted homosexual, and Patrick hates himself.

He says he was sexually abused by his father at age four. He claims to have been a prostitute at age sixteen. There are rumors that he has molested young boys. His history is nebulous.

He tells me that he is no good, and that there is no place for him – even the homosexual community doesn't want him. He is suicidal.

Asked to name only one good thing about himself, he can't. A fellow patient tells him he has a beautiful smile and a good sense of humor. He smiles coyly at this and seems quite pleased. But it doesn't dispel the cloak of doom he wears.

He talks of "bad thoughts." One can only guess what they are and pity him, as he has to deal with the demons that drive him.

Earnest

He grins a wide, gap-toothed grin. He speaks very loudly, spraying saliva on the recipients of his attention. He continues to talk, even after his listener has left, and begins to repeat what he has just said.

After a gentle reminder to speak more softly, he grins again and tries. Soon, his loud harsh voice is heard up once again up and down the halls.

He is tall, black, and very muscular. His gentle nature belies his booming voice and intimidating outward appearance.

Natalie

A pale, slim 16-year-old has returned to our hospital. Three days in the real world were too much for her. The fragile line between sanity and insanity had been crossed.

She envisioned narcotics on the table of our lounge, then went to her room and took a shower with her clothes on.

Poor, frail, Natalie. Will she ever be able to deal with real life?

Robert

He comes to us with a sad face. He is really low. He hates himself so much that he tried to smash his foot with a board, and he snapped a mousetrap on his penis.

He seems like a reasonable guy, with a supportive wife and daughter.

Why doesn't he like himself?

Bob

When Bob is admitted to our unit, I think to myself, "That is the strangest human being I have ever seen."

He has a very round head, and his hair looks like it was cut around a bowl. His dark hair is plastered down (by his own hand), and arranged neatly in little tendrils, like Julius Caesar. His face is round, and very red. He is fat, especially around the middle, and he wears his "high-water" pants hiked up to his rib cage.

He eyes a group of ladies suspiciously, and asks why they are laughing at him. He tells us he is going to dig his eyes out, and do various other things to his body. He hoards things in his room. Anything he gets his hands on is squirreled away in one of his drawers.

Beulah

She's a big girl – at least 5'10", and quite strong. She has light brown skin, and her hair sits on top of her head like a mushroom.

She has very little self-control, and when one of her fellow patients is rude to her, she attacks him mercilessly. He is a tiny whip of a guy, tough, but no match for her.

She barely gets her hands on him, when several staff members intervene to hold her back. Kicking, screaming, and fighting, she is restrained.

John

Sometimes in life, things happen that are so heartbreaking that you would like to have no memory of the tragedy.

On this night, a man named John is brought into our unit by police and staff. I've never seen anyone so miserable. He is screaming, yelling, and crying. His arms flail and legs kick. He is taken into our unit and given an injection to calm him down.

Staff is gathered and informed that he had accidentally shot and killed his son. They had been hunting and gotten separated. We assumed he thought the movement in the bushes was a deer.

My heart fills with compassion for him. Will he ever be at peace?

Afterword

"There, but for the grace of God, go I."

As I cared for my patients, that phrase gained new meaning. There is much in life that is beyond our control—the family that we are born into and the many ways it shapes us. Sometimes the challenges of life become more than we are prepared to deal with alone, and my psychiatric patients were not unique in this.

The days I spent working with them strengthened my own faith. I felt a sense of God's love for all His children—my patients and their wounded families, the medical professionals who cared for them, and the forest that grew outside our hospital walls, providing a path for healing.

Like the trees and wildflowers that grew there, we are connected. We were meant to be so.

This, I believe, is the essence of our humanity. We are one family. And, together, we will adapt to our environment.

Acknowledgements

I would like to acknowledge my editor and illustrator, Carmel Mawle, who encouraged and aided me. Without her guidance, I would never have finished or published these "Portraits."

About the Author

Nancy Johnson is the author of *Letters from Egypt: Four Years of Family Life Beneath The Pyramids* and *In Gratitude for Life, Love, Family & Friends: A Collection of Essays and Poems*.

The daughter of a naval officer, Nancy lived in many places as a child. She married a petroleum engineer and lived in many more places.

Nancy was a teacher and later earned a degree in nursing.

www.ingramcontent.com/pod-product-compliance
Lightning Source LLC
Chambersburg PA
CBHW071255070526
44583CB00017B/2476